Six Simple Ways
to Assess
Young Children

Early Childhood Education
providing lessons for life

www.EarlyChildEd.delmar.com

Six Simple Ways to Assess Young Children

Sue Gober, Ed.D.

DELMAR

THOMSON LEARNING Australia · Canada · Mexico · Singapore · Spain · United Kingdom · United States

Six Simple Ways to Assess Young Children
by Sue Gober, Ed. D.

Business Unit Director:
Susan L. Simpfenderfer

Executive Production Manager:
Wendy A. Troeger

Executive Marketing Manager:
Donna J. Lewis

Executive Editor:
Marlene McHugh Pratt

Project Editor:
Amy E. Tucker

Channel Manager:
Nigar Hale

Acquisitions Editor:
Erin O'Connor Traylor

Production Editor:
J.P. Henkel

Cover Design:
Joe Villanova

Editorial Assistant:
Alexis Ferraro

For permission to use material from this text or product, contact us by
Tel   (800) 730-2214
Fax   (800) 730-2215
www.thomsonrights.com

Library of Congress Cataloging-in-Publication Data

Gober, Sue.
   Six simple ways to assess young children / Sue Gober.
      p. cm.
   Includes bibliographical references and index.
   ISBN 978-0-7668-3925-0
   ISBN 0-7668-3925-7
   1. Educational tests and measurements. 2. Students--Rating of.
3. Early childhood education.   I. Title.
   LB3060.217 .G63 2001
   372.126--dc21
                                          2001032457

NOTICE TO THE READER

Publisher does not warrant or guarantee any of the products described herein or perform any independent analysis in connection with any of the product information contained herein. Publisher does not assume, and expressly disclaims, any obligation to obtain and include information other than that provided to it by the manufacturer.

The reader is expressly warned to consider and adopt all safety precautions that might be indicated by the activities herein and to avoid all potential hazards. By following the instructions contained herein, the reader willingly assumes all risks in connection with such instructions.

The Publisher makes no representation or warranties of any kind, including but not limited to, the warranties of fitness for particular purpose or merchantability, nor are any such representations implied with respect to the material set forth herein, and the publisher takes no responsibility with respect to such material. The publisher shall not be liable for any special, consequential, or exemplary damages resulting, in whole or part, from the readers' use of, or reliance upon, this material.

This book is dedicated to
Dr. Lee Mountain, professor at the University of Houston.

During my doctoral work at the university, I chose to take the publication course everyone raved about. I gained a new appreciation for writing when I entered that classroom and met Dr. Lee Mountain. She possessed such an excitement and enthusiasm for writing that her contagious spirit caught fire during that semester. This book is a result of a book proposal assignment written for that class. She inspired me to write and put my ideas on paper because she believed that I had something to offer. I have enjoyed this endeavor and hope many teachers utilize the assessment techniques that I have personally enjoyed using during my teaching years. Thank you, Dr. Mountain, for being such an inspiration to so many, and thank you for believing in me. You are truly one-of-a-kind.

-Sue Gober

Contents

Part 2

Part 3

Appendices

Preface

Purpose of the Book

In the field of education, accountability has become a buzzword. That simply means that teachers must find ways to show that children are learning. State boards of education are demanding proof that children are mastering specific objectives for each age group.

In early childhood education, the same accountability holds true. Teachers of young children must find ways to show that children from birth through age eight are growing, developing, and learning. Parents, as well as teachers, want to see proof of growth and development. Appropriate assessment methods, such as those discussed in *Six Simple Ways to Assess Young Children*, can provide that proof.

Need for the Book

There are many assessment books on the market today, but few are easy to read with "how-to" details on specific methods. Many teachers of young children have little or no college training, and in fact may have very little training at all. In child care centers, teachers without formal training or skills can be hired. Despite the varying degree of teacher preparation that exists, it is important that all teachers of young children understand the need for assessment in the classroom setting. How else will we know that children are learning?

Who Will Benefit from this Book?

Beginning teachers, as well as veterans who care for children in child care centers, nursery school programs, and day homes will find this book helpful. Because it spells out methods so that anyone can understand, this book can be implemented immediately to evaluate young children in meaningful ways. No further explanations are needed.

Many of my friends are teaching kindergarten in public schools, but expressed a desire to learn how to build a portfolio. They are required to give one-shot tests, but want to know how to show growth and development over time. This portfolio approach demonstrates that.

Pre-service teachers (college students) want a blueprint for everything they are learning in education classes. *Six Simple Ways to Assess Young Children* can also serve as a supplement to a college text because it spells out assessment without the "intellectual college jargon." That's what teachers, *all* teachers, really want—a book that can be understood and implemented quickly by anyone.

Contents

This practical, easy-to-read book, explores the topic of assessment for young children, and examines six specific assessment methods currently used by many teachers in the field. Credibility is established for these methods as they have been implemented successfully over and over again. They may not seem new or magical to some, but in this context, they are clearly explained through common-sense ideas and are easy to follow.

Six Simple Ways to Assess Young Children is teacher-friendly and easy to read, divided into three sections. Part 1 is an introduction to assessment that defines and explains current, fundamental terms that all teachers must know. It answers the following teacher questions.

1. What does it really mean when I say, "How can I assess the children in my classroom?"

2. Why should I spend my time and effort assessing children each year?

3. Can assessment be simplified and really become "doable?"

Part 2 shares specifics by explaining the six simple assessment tools. The first method of assessment is a checklist based on developmental milestones. The five methods following the checklist include parent interviews, self-portraits, work samples, audio (or video) tapes, and anecdotal record-keeping of observations.

All six methods are described in detail, include examples, and can be used as stand-alone assessments if desired. Teachers do not need to implement all six methods, but rather choose one or two that they feel comfortable with. One suggestion is to become familiar with the behaviors on the checklist. Then, choose any of the other five methods to document those behaviors over time.

Each assessment method addresses the questions: what, who, where, when how, and why and is illustrated with photographs, points to remember, and supporting forms. A Teacher Talk section wraps up each discussion with quotes from teachers' experiences using each assessment method at various age groups.

Part 3 gives suggestions on how to create a storage system for the information that is collected over the course of the year. One popular way to store information and materials gathered on each child is through the use of a portfolio. This section includes a complete explanation of the portfolio including the use of an end-of-year narrative summary. Assessment for children with special needs is also discussed in this section.

The four appendices provide examples of parent interview forms, developmental checklists, samples of anecdotal records, and an example of a narrative summary together in an organized fashion. Although these examples are located in each part, the author felt that it would be helpful if they were also located together in the appendices.

Some may find that each section stands alone and can be used separately at any time. Others will use all the information provided, to better and more accurately understand assessment of their young students. Hopefully, the book answers questions about assessment of the children you teach and gives simple, exact methods to implement in your classroom immediately. All child care and preschool teachers, with varying levels of formal training, must assess their students. This book helps by simplifying six methods of assessment available to all teachers of young children.

*A*cknowledgments

I would like to thank Vassar College for contributions to this book along with the teachers, parents, and director of Lamar University's Early Childhood Development Center, including:

Lori Graham, Director	Dee Ann Kelly
Dauphine Arbuckle	Barbara Merriam
Lisa Bailey	Jessica Robbins
Susan Caffarel	Pam Sahualla
Lori Eller	Amy Underwood

Without their help, support, discussions, and input, this book would never have been completed. They provided classroom examples and experiences dealing with real, child assessment issues. I will be forever grateful for their assistance.

Reviewers

The author and Delmar would like to thank the following reviewers whose feedback helped shape this valuable resource into a readily-usable format.

Angela Buchanan
DeAnza College
Cupertino, CA

Kathy Fite
Southwest Texas State University
San Marcos, TX

Amber Tankersley
Missouri Southern State College
Joplin, MO

Sandra Wanner
University of Mary Hardin-Baylor
Belton, TX

PART 1

Assessment—

The Art of Making

It Simple

An Introduction

Recently, I was asked to present a workshop on assessment methods for young children at a state conference. As the presentation was about to begin, I noticed the room was overflowing with teachers of all ages eager to know more about assessment. I asked each of them to write one question or concern they had about assessment. The following questions were generated from that workshop audience.

- How can I pull it all together—the goals, portfolios, evaluations, curriculum, and planning?
- How can I help parents understand my evaluations?
- What should I cover in my observations so that I don't just write down problems?
- What does NAEYC offer on the most current methods of evaluation?
- What should be included in a portfolio, and how often should I update it?
- How can the portfolio idea really become "doable?"
- How can I simplify assessment?
- What are the "hows" and "whys" of assessment?
- What assessment methods are best for each age group?

During that brief session, I attempted the impossible task of answering their questions and concerns (Figure 1–1). When the workshop ended, I

Figure 1–1 Teachers of all ages and experience levels have questions about assessment.

realized if those teachers had so many basic concerns about assessment issues, others must have the same questions as well. This book was written in an attempt to provide basic information for teachers about classroom assessment.

Definition of Assessment

Assessment can mean different things to different people. The dictionary defines assessment as "taking stock of a situation." In this book, I will use the term *assessment* to mean exactly that same notion. Teachers are required to evaluate the children they teach and *take stock* of their growth and development (Figure 1–2). Of course, there are many types of assessments or evaluations that can be implemented with children, such as standardized tests, rating scales, check sheets, numerical grades, letter grades, portfolios, observations, and many more.

Authentic assessment is a term currently used by teachers when discussing the best ways to take stock, or evaluate, student progress. **Authentic assessment** can be defined as the process of documenting and evaluating growth and development, over time, using real-life situations. It shows what children can do, what they know, and what they understand. It is *not* a one-shot,

Figure 1–2 Teachers are required to evaluate children and keep documented records of their assessments.

Figure 1–3 Teachers can learn a lot about children from observing them play.

one-time test. Teachers are beginning to realize that this type of performance assessment gives a more accurate picture of who the child is, and how the child is growing and learning.

The term *assessment*, when used in the context of early childhood education, is sometimes interchanged with the term, *observation*. **Observation** is one method of assessing student growth and development and is probably the best-known, most widely used way that teachers evaluate the progress of the young children they teach (Figure 1–3).

What Should I Assess?

Teachers often wonder what behaviors, skills, or activities are important for observation and documentation. Many use a report card, or simple checklist of behaviors, to communicate to a parent how the child is doing in the classroom. Sometimes the choice of using only one method does not reveal an accurate picture of the child—and may even imply an incorrect message. There are alternatives to traditional methods that are more in tune with the child's natural growth and development as it occurs on a daily basis.

One alternative assessment tool is a **portfolio approach** that allows the teacher to document behaviors and skills focused on the developmental milestones of the child's age group. **Developmental milestones** are overall basic skills or accomplishments that most children have or can do at a particular age or stage. If you have never assessed children, developmental milestones provide a place to start that process and later become the focus of your teaching and assessment practices. These are not detailed, daily curriculum objectives or teaching goals, but they do provide an overview of what children should know or be able to accomplish.

The first assessment method, which is discussed in Part 2, is a **developmental checklist** for each age group. The other five assessment techniques following the checklists can be used to document the skills and behaviors included in those checklists. My six simple ways to assess young children include explanations of

1. developmental checklists

2. parent interviews

3. self-portraits

4. scribbling, drawing, and writing samples

5. audio or video tapes

6. anecdotal records

It is extremely important for teachers to first understand the developmental milestones for the age of children in the classroom. When completing the checklist for a child, it is imperative to have documentation showing that the child has mastered each skill or area. The assessment methods following the developmental checklists will suggest helpful, easy ways to do that. As the teacher, you can choose one or several approaches to help document the growth of children in your classroom. The methods chosen can be determined by the

1. amount of time the teacher has available for assessment.

2. availability of extra help from an assistant, aide, or volunteer.

3. support of the administration or director of the program.

Developmental Milestones

There are four basic areas included in the developmental milestones.

■ **Physical Growth/Motor Development**—This area refers to the child's actual physical (body) growth as he/she gains ability to move and control body parts (Figure 1–4).

■ **Social/Personal Development**—This area refers to the child's development of social skills, or the ability to interact with others (Figure 1–5). It also includes how the children feel about themselves.

Figure 1–4 This child's developing motor skills enable her to balance on one foot.

Figure 1–5 As a child's social/personal development advances, he becomes more comfortable interacting in groups.

Figure 1–6 Young children give little thought to expressing their true feelings.

■ **Emotional Development/Feelings**—This area refers to the child's growth and development of feelings and how they are expressed (Figure 1–6). Self-esteem is also part of this area of development.

■ **Cognitive/Language Development**—This area refers to the child's mental growth and development, which includes language. The word *cognitive* means thinking; therefore, how a child thinks is an indicator of development (Figure 1–7). Most children express thinking skills through language.

It is important to evaluate the whole child, not just one part. Although it appears easier to look at one developmental area at a time in order to simplify assessment, all areas are dependent on each other and should be intertwined. The methods chosen for assessment should include documentation of *all* areas of development.

The checklist includes all developmental milestones and can be used as a guide for what to assess. Teachers can add or delete skills if desired. These lists were compiled from many sources, but are not inclusive. The six assessment methods explained in *Six Simple Ways to Assess Young Children* can be used to document those specific skills listed in the checklists. Developmental checklists for each age group are repeated in the appendices.

At the end of the school year, it will be the job of the teacher to pull the assessment methods together into a **narrative summary**, which paints a picture of the child's growth and development. A checklist does not give the

Figure 1–7 Cognitive development is demonstrated through the thought processes involved in working a puzzle.

specific, personal comments a teacher wants to share with parents. The narrative summary will show where the children started in the beginning of the school year and where they are at the end of the year. The information can be placed in a file folder and passed to the next teacher (Figure 1–8). The work saved in the portfolio can be given to the parents for documentation.

Figure 1–8 A child's narrative summary provides insight for both parents and future teachers.

Before choosing one or more assessment methods, be sure to read and understand the developmental milestones. You should feel confident that your methods will help you see the "whole child," so that all developmental areas can be documented for **growth**.

Why Assess Young Children?

Early childhood includes children from birth to age eight and is a very difficult period to assess because the rate of growth is so rapid. Also, growth is highly influenced by nurturing parents, quality of care, and the learning environment. Parents want to be assured, however, that their child is ready for school. In addition, teachers and administrators want to know if they are offering effective programs. Therefore, assessment information is critical to the child, the parent, and the success of the program.

During the 90s, President George Bush set National Education Goals to assure that all children would start school "ready to learn." The **National Education Goals Panel** was asked to create recommendations regarding the purposes of early childhood assessment. A summary of the purposes for assessment of young children, set by the National Education Goals Panel (1998), includes the following information.

The number one reason to assess young children is to benefit the child. If the assessment is tied closely to instruction, it will be easier for the teacher to see what and how the child is learning.

■ Teachers must assess to identify children for special services. When ongoing assessments are implemented, teachers become aware of issues to be addressed (Figure 1–9).

Figure 1–9 Assessment helps teachers identify children with special needs.

■ Large scale monitoring of data can provide information regarding current trends, programs, and services.

■ Academic achievement must be assessed to hold students, teachers, and schools accountable (Figure 1–10). High-stakes testing is becoming popular nationwide to identify where learning is taking place; but there should be no formal testing until the end of third grade. Assessments should be performance-based, documenting growth over time with appropriate methods.

The **National Association for the Education of Young Children (NAEYC)** offers reasons to assess children as well. As one of the most respected professional organizations for early childhood educators, they endorse the beliefs that assessments should be conducted in a developmentally-appropriate manner. They also maintain that assessment helps teachers plan instruction for individual students, can be used to identify children who need special services, and can be used to evaluate a whole program on how well goals are being met.

NAEYC publishes guidelines for assessment that can be used in implementing authentic assessment practices (Bredekamp & Rosegrant, 1992). A few major points of those guidelines include:

■ Assessment and curriculum must be integrated. If you assess your children for what they know and can do, it will help you decide what you should be teaching.

■ All areas of development should be assessed in order to capture an accurate picture of the "whole child."

Figure 1–10 Academic assessment helps keep teachers and schools accountable, as well as the children.

Figure 1–11 Samples of children's writing, art, and school work should be saved to document progress.

■ Assessment should be ongoing and over time, with a systematic collection of samples (Figure 1–11).

■ Assessment can use a variety of tools and processes, such as collections of work, recordings, interviews, and anecdotal records.

■ Assessment occurs during typical daily activities.

■ Assessment should demonstrate what a child can do alone and with assistance (Figure 1–12).

■ Teachers should report meaningful, descriptive information to parents.

NAEYC believes that we must have knowledge of individual children and child development, as well as an understanding of diversity in order to prepare our classrooms and curriculum for young children (Shores & Grace, 1998). This book shares methods to help meet those objectives. A more detailed listing of NAEYC guidelines can be found in *Reaching Potentials: Appropriate Curriculum and Assessment for Young Children* (1992) edited by Sue Bredekamp and Teresa Rosegrant.

How Should Young Children Be Assessed?

While teaching kindergarten at the Lamar University Early Childhood Development Center, I felt the frustration of first grade teachers, in the local school districts, looking for a test score to place children according to academic ability. I gave in to the pressure, and tried a paper and pencil test at the end of the kindergarten year. It was an eye-opening experience about

Figure 1–12 Observation helps assess what children can accomplish on their own and with assistance.

formal testing of young children! After three children sobbed uncontrollably, because they had to work alone and could not talk to their friends, I made a definite commitment to never again use formal group testing for my entire class of kindergarten students (Figure 1–13).

I learned by trial and error that assessment could not be a one-time test, but must be a year-long process that includes developmentally appropriate methods such as observations, collection of children's work, parent interviews, and other methods to collectively show an accurate, visual picture of the child (Figure 1–14). That one-time test score could not possibly tell the first grade teacher everything about a child from my kindergarten class.

Children can represent their knowledge better by physically showing or doing than by writing in a test booklet. When children show what they know, it is called **performance-based** (or **authentic**) **assessment**. I found this type of assessment to be a *process*, not a *product*. Even though the narrative summary at the end of the year might be considered a *product*, it is the *process* of arriving at the summary that is important in understanding a child.

Figure 1–13 An eight-year-old will respond more favorably to formal assessment methods than a five-year-old.

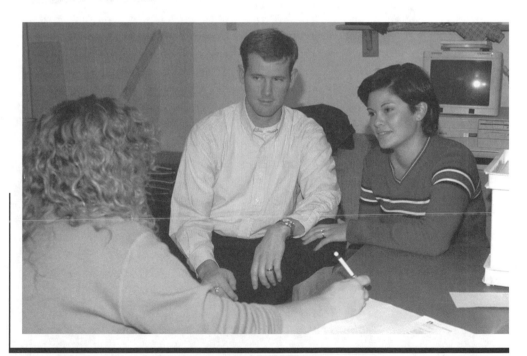

Figure 1–14 Parent interviews can provide valuable information about a child for both the parents and teacher.

Summary

Assessment is a hot topic in the field of early childhood education as accountability becomes more important for teachers and schools. As educators, we must find ways to show we are teaching and that children are learning. It is imperative to find methods that illustrate growth and development over time, allowing children to be evaluated in real-life, everyday settings. It is the teachers' responsibility to find methods of documentation that report successes of children. Teachers must look at what children can do, not spend valuable assessment time finding all of the things they cannot do.

By understanding the basic developmental areas of the children you teach, assessment can be made simple. The following easy-to-learn methods will help you document developmental growth of young children over time.

PART 2

Six Methods
of Assessment

ASSESSMENT METHOD 1:
Developmental Checklists

What can I do to assess young children?

One method of assessment is using a checklist.

DEVELOPMENTAL CHECKLIST
0–12 Months

	Observed	Not Observed
Physical Growth/Motor Development		
Looks around (2 months)	☐	☐
Laughs aloud (3–5 months)	☐	☐
Controls head movements (about 4 months)	☐	☐
Notices hands/feet and plays with them (3–5 months)	☐	☐
Rolls over (4–6 months)	☐	☐
Sits up without support (6–8 months)	☐	☐
Holds bottle (6–8 months)	☐	☐
Crawls (6–8 months)	☐	☐
Walks with support	☐	☐
Imitates adults' facial gestures	☐	☐
Reaches, grasps	☐	☐
Puts objects in mouth (Figure 2–3)	☐	☐
Picks things up with thumb and finger	☐	☐
Picks up toys that are dropped	☐	☐
Teeth appear (6–12 months)	☐	☐

Figure 2–3 As infants' motor skills advance, they begin putting objects in their mouths.

	Observed	Not Observed
Social/Personal Development		
Smiles spontaneously (0–3 months)	☐	☐
Recognizes mother	☐	☐
Begins to notice strangers	☐	☐
Enjoys personal play and contact	☐	☐
Vocalizes, squeals with joy (Figure 2–4)	☐	☐
Imitates actions	☐	☐
Participates in "peek-a-boo" and other games	☐	☐
May cry when left alone	☐	☐

Figure 2–4 Children from 0–12 months will often smile or squeal with joy.

Figure 2–1 Developmental checklists help gauge a child's progress.

Complete a checklist of developmental skills on each child.

Who needs a checklist?

Children from birth to age eight need checklists performed to document development.

Developmental milestones
- help teachers and parents know and understand children.
- will vary for different age groups and stages of development.

Where will this activity take place?

This activity can take place anywhere, any time!

This is a great activity to complete during rest time, when you have quiet time to think about the child's growth and development.

When should I complete a checklist on each child?

A checklist should be completed three times during the year.

Checklists should be completed in the
- fall.
- winter.
- spring.

How do I complete a checklist?

To complete a checklist make a copy of the checklist on pages 25–38 (or Appendix A), purchase one, or make your own.

Checklists should always

- be objective.
- contain the dates of observation.
- document the child's skills using other assessment techniques such as work samples, audio tapes, or anecdotal records as well.

*W*hy should I complete a developmental checklist on each child?

It provides a good overall assessment tool (Figure 2–2).

Figure 2–2 Checklists provide objective documentation of a child's growth and development.

A checklist

- is quick and easy to use.
- can be used to report growth and development to parents during the year.
- is objective.
- acts as a guide so that important areas are easily documented.
- gives an overall picture of what a child should know and be able to do at a certain age.

Teachers share their thoughts and experiences surrounding assessment methods used with children of various age levels.

18-months–2 ½-year-olds

> ❝I send a checklist home every two months. These children grow so fast; it has been helpful for parents to see what they are learning.❞

4-year-olds

> ❝I have used developmental checklists for years. Parents seem to find them easy to follow. I found this year that I wanted to document the skills listed on the checklist. I tried to save work samples to show how and what a child was learning. It was great to make the connection between the developmental milestones and my classroom activities. I felt more confident sending home the checklists.❞

Understanding Developmental Checklists

- The developmental milestones listed in the sample developmental checklists that follow are broad skills intended to give an overall picture of children in specific age groups.

- You will discover that some skills belong in more than one area of development.

- Children grow and change rapidly from birth to age eight. Become familiar with the broad developmental milestones, understanding that all children develop at different rates.

- Do not use the checklist as a report card of strengths and weaknesses, but as a guide for normal development.

- The checklist can be a discussion tool for development by making notes or comments about specific characteristics. This is helpful when talking to parents.

- Use the checklist as you make anecdotal records. It will serve as a guide for the four broad areas of development.

- You can add or delete skills. There is an endless list of characteristics and skills for each age group. You decide how detailed you want your list.

DEVELOPMENTAL CHECKLIST
0–12 Months

	Observed	Not Observed

Physical Growth/Motor Development

	Observed	Not Observed
Looks around (2 months)	☐	☐
Laughs aloud (3–5 months)	☐	☐
Controls head movements (about 4 months)	☐	☐
Notices hands/feet and plays with them (3–5 months)	☐	☐
Rolls over (4–6 months)	☐	☐
Sits up without support (6–8 months)	☐	☐
Holds bottle (6–8 months)	☐	☐
Crawls (6–8 months)	☐	☐
Walks with support	☐	☐
Imitates adults' facial gestures	☐	☐
Reaches, grasps	☐	☐
Puts objects in mouth (Figure 2–3)	☐	☐
Picks things up with thumb and finger	☐	☐
Picks up toys that are dropped	☐	☐
Teeth appear (6–12 months)	☐	☐

Figure 2–3 As infants' motor skills advance, they begin putting objects in their mouths.

Social/Personal Development

	Observed	Not Observed
Smiles spontaneously (0–3 months)	☐	☐
Recognizes mother	☐	☐
Begins to notice strangers	☐	☐
Enjoys personal play and contact	☐	☐
Vocalizes, squeals with joy (Figure 2–4)	☐	☐
Imitates actions	☐	☐
Participates in "peek-a-boo" and other games	☐	☐
May cry when left alone	☐	☐

Figure 2–4 Children from 0–12 months will often smile or squeal with joy.

	Observed	Not Observed

Cognitive/Language Development

	Observed	Not Observed
Responds to different sounds/voices	☐	☐
Studies and inspects things for long periods of time	☐	☐
Notices if you hide an object	☐	☐
Becomes curious	☐	☐
Learns and responds to "no"	☐	☐
Follows object with eyes (Figure 2–5)	☐	☐
Imitates others	☐	☐
Puts objects in and out of containers	☐	☐

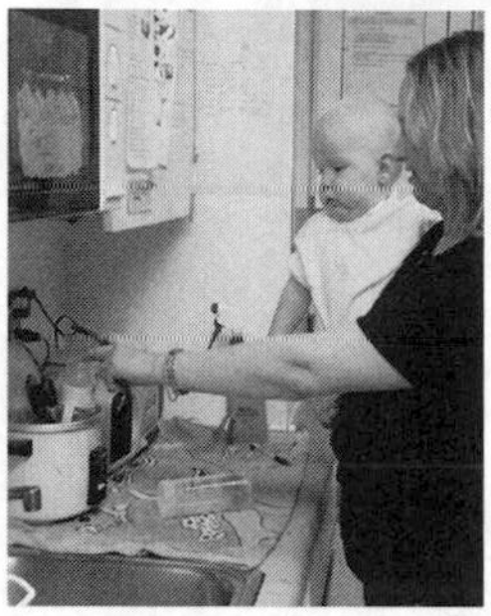

Figure 2–5 This infant watches his teacher prepare his bottle.

Emotional Development/Feelings

	Observed	Not Observed
Smiles	☐	☐
Squeals with joy and pleasure	☐	☐
Cries differently for hunger, pain, cold, wet (Figure 2–6)	☐	☐
Shows fear by using body movements	☐	☐
Shows affection	☐	☐
Begins to show anger (9–14 months)	☐	☐

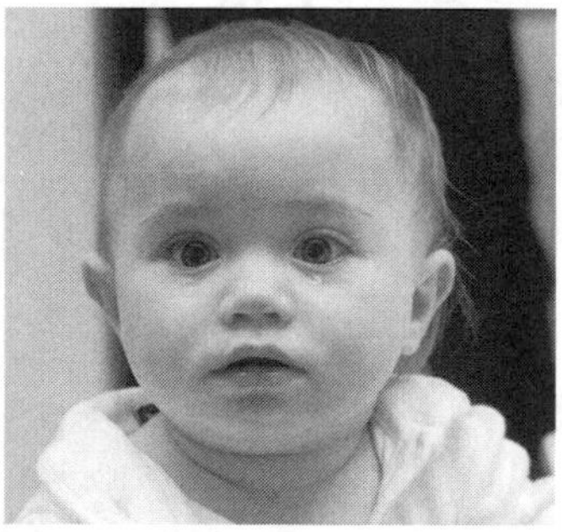

Figure 2–6 Tears on an infant can mean hunger, pain, or a diaper needs changing.

DEVELOPMENTAL CHECKLIST
12–24 Months

	Observed	Not Observed

Physical Growth/Motor Development

	Observed	Not Observed
Teething continues	☐	☐
Crawls well, stands alone well	☐	☐
Walks without help	☐	☐
Pushes, pulls toys	☐	☐
Sits in chair	☐	☐
Moves to music	☐	☐
Throws, kicks a ball	☐	☐
Crawls down stairs backward	☐	☐
Stacks blocks	☐	☐
Uses a spoon, chews food	☐	☐
Turns book pages	☐	☐
Jumps up and down	☐	☐
Holds glass (Figure 2–7)	☐	☐
Opens doors and cabinets	☐	☐
Scribbles, paints with whole arm	☐	☐
Starts elimination control	☐	☐

Figure 2–7 Children between one and two years begin to hold their own spoons and bottles during feeding.

Social/Personal Development

	Observed	Not Observed
Recognizes self in mirror (Figure 2–8)	☐	☐
Understands own name and responds	☐	☐
Initiates play	☐	☐
Imitates adults	☐	☐
Helps pick up toys	☐	☐
Identifies body parts	☐	☐
Shows interest in playing with peers, enjoys others	☐	☐
Becomes possessive	☐	☐

Figure 2–8 Toddlers enjoy seeing their reflection in a mirror.

	Observed	Not Observed

Cognitive/Language Development

	Observed	Not Observed
Talks, words accompany gestures	☐	☐
Responds to simple directions	☐	☐
Begins to put words together	☐	☐
Enjoys rhythm and rhyme	☐	☐
Likes to hear same story over again (Figure 2–9)	☐	☐
Takes apart and puts back together	☐	☐
Looks for hidden objects	☐	☐
Shows signs of memory development	☐	☐
Solves problems through trial and error	☐	☐

Figure 2–9 A two-year-old never tires of hearing her favorite story repeated.

Emotional Development/Feelings

	Observed	Not Observed
Begins to show shame, guilt, shyness	☐	☐
Shows frustrations	☐	☐
May show moods (Figure 2–10)	☐	☐
May rebel, resist, run away	☐	☐
Humor develops	☐	☐
Can be negative, says no	☐	☐
Laughs, shows joy	☐	☐

Figure 2–10 As the child's emotional development matures, he may begin to show various moods.

DEVELOPMENTAL CHECKLIST
24–36 Months

	Observed	Not Observed

Physical Growth/Motor Development

	Observed	Not Observed
Uses a spoon without spilling	☐	☐
Opens doors	☐	☐
Puts on coat	☐	☐
Washes and dries hands	☐	☐
Begins to cut with scissors (Figure 2–11)	☐	☐
Uses one hand consistently	☐	☐
Runs forward, jumps in place, climbs	☐	☐
Stands on one foot	☐	☐
Walks on tiptoes	☐	☐
Kicks ball forward	☐	☐
Rides a tricycle	☐	☐
Marches to music	☐	☐

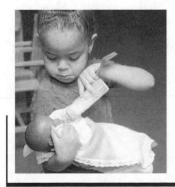

Figure 2–11 This child is developing fine motor skills by learning to manipulate scissors.

Social/Personal Development

	Observed	Not Observed
Uses words for wants and seeks teacher attention	☐	☐
Plays near others, then begins to play with others (in groups of 2 or 3 children)	☐	☐
Watches other children	☐	☐
Participates in group activities	☐	☐
Understands gender identity	☐	☐
Helpful	☐	☐
Shows independence (Figure 2–12)	☐	☐
May have imaginary playmates	☐	☐

Figure 2–12 Two- to three-year-olds often show their independence through dramatic play.

	Observed	Not Observed

Cognitive/Language Development

	Observed	Not Observed
Uses words to express wants, makes sentences, answers yes/no questions	☐	☐
Begins counting (Figure 2–13)	☐	☐
Responds and follows directions	☐	☐
Matches similar objects	☐	☐
Enjoys books	☐	☐
Recognizes differences in you and me	☐	☐
Gaining attention span	☐	☐
Explores world, very curious, asks questions	☐	☐
Can tell you what he/she is doing	☐	☐
Stacks rings according to size, attempts 2- and 3-piece puzzles	☐	☐
Gives first and last name	☐	☐
Asks "what" and "where" questions	☐	☐
Shows interest in toilet training	☐	☐

Figure 2–13 Birthdays help children begin to associate numbers and counting.

Emotional Development/Feelings

	Observed	Not Observed
May show fears	☐	☐
Intentional lying may begin (closer to age three)	☐	☐
Shows pride	☐	☐
Uses words for emotions, shows sympathy and affection	☐	☐
Feelings can be hurt	☐	☐
Associates facial expressions with emotions (Figure 2–14)	☐	☐
Shows temper	☐	☐

Figure 2–14 Using facial expressions to convey emotions is common to this age group.

DEVELOPMENTAL CHECKLIST
3-Year-Olds

	Observed	Not Observed

Physical Growth/Motor Development

	Observed	Not Observed
Copies circles	☐	☐
Manipulates clay, puzzles, scissors (Figure 2–15)	☐	☐
Builds	☐	☐
Runs around obstacles	☐	☐
Walks on a line	☐	☐
Hops/balances on one foot	☐	☐
Steers and pedals tricycle	☐	☐
Throws ball overhand	☐	☐
Jumps with two feet	☐	☐
Begins to use zippers/buttons to dress	☐	☐

Figure 2–15 By age three, children have a better command of fine motor skills.

Social/Personal Development

	Observed	Not Observed
Tells name	☐	☐
May continue to play alongside others or join in the play	☐	☐
Shares, takes turns (may have difficulty with this)	☐	☐
Identifies others	☐	☐
Sings (Figure 2–16)	☐	☐
Accepts responsibility/demonstrates self-control	☐	☐
Begins dramatic play/pretends	☐	☐

Figure 2–16 This child's bold singing demonstrates her personal and social development.

	Observed	Not Observed
Cognitive/Language Development		
Solves problems	☐	☐
Listens attentively	☐	☐
Follows simple directions	☐	☐
Completes task	☐	☐
Can express self verbally	☐	☐
Compares size (Figure 2–17)	☐	☐
Counts	☐	☐
Recognizes and matches colors	☐	☐
Draws picture, can explain it to an adult	☐	☐
Asks "why" questions	☐	☐
Knows name, age	☐	☐
Has short attention span	☐	☐
Can group objects	☐	☐
Talks in sentences	☐	☐
Begins to understand time concepts	☐	☐
Refers to self as "I" or "me"	☐	☐
Speech is understandable, using sentences	☐	☐

Figure 2–17 As cognitive skills develop, children learn to group objects and compare sizes.

	Observed	Not Observed
Emotional Development/Feelings		
Is developing self-confidence (Figure 2–18)	☐	☐
Expresses feelings in an appropriate manner	☐	☐
Accepts constructive criticism	☐	☐
Developing humor, may be silly	☐	☐
Can revert to toddler behavior of sucking thumb, crying, etc., if unhappy	☐	☐

Figure 2–18 A confident three-year-old may attempt to read along with the teacher.

DEVELOPMENTAL CHECKLIST
4-Year-Olds

	Observed	Not Observed
Physical Growth/Motor Development		
Draws, paints, uses scissors	☐	☐
Dresses and undresses without assistance (Figure 2–19)	☐	☐
Walks stairs alone, alternating feet	☐	☐
Self-reliant in bathroom	☐	☐
Kicks, throws, bounces, catches a ball	☐	☐
Runs, hops, skips, jumps, gallops	☐	☐
Developing eye-hand coordination	☐	☐

Figure 2–19 Four-year-olds can typically dress themselves.

	Observed	Not Observed
Social/Personal Development		
Plays and interacts with others	☐	☐
Dramatic play is close to reality, using detail (Figure 2–20)	☐	☐
Shows interest in gender differences	☐	☐
Tries new things	☐	☐
Participates/functions well in group activities	☐	☐
Works and plays well with others	☐	☐
Uses table manners	☐	☐
Respects property of others	☐	☐
Able to resolve minor conflicts	☐	☐
Accepts authority	☐	☐

Figure 2–20 These girls mimic real-life in their dramatic play experiences.

	Observed	Not Observed

Cognitive/Language Development

	Observed	Not Observed
Counts	☐	☐
Interested in letters and sounds (beginning reading skills)	☐	☐
Good listener	☐	☐
Follows directions	☐	☐
Makes decisions or choices	☐	☐
Sees the connection between effort and accomplishment	☐	☐
Can complete a task without distractions (Figure 2–21)	☐	☐
Works independently, will ask for help	☐	☐
Strives to get things right	☐	☐
Likes to learn		

Figure 2–21 By age four, a child's focus enables him to stay on task.

Emotional Development/Feelings

	Observed	Not Observed
Feels secure away from familiar surroundings	☐	☐
Accepts mistakes	☐	☐
Expresses individual thoughts and feelings	☐	☐
Separates easily from parents (Figure 2–22)	☐	☐
Develops self-confidence	☐	☐
Greater ability to control anger/fear	☐	☐

Figure 2–22 This child exhibits no fear and loneliness when his parent must leave.

DEVELOPMENTAL CHECKLIST
5-Year-Olds

	Observed	Not Observed

Physical Growth/Motor Development

	Observed	Not Observed
Takes care of personal needs (ties shoes, buttons, zips, etc)	☐	☐
Coordinates body parts (biking, swimming, etc.)	☐	☐
Cuts accurately	☐	☐
Uses pencil and scissors correctly (Figure 2–23)	☐	☐
Basic grasp of right and left, but confuses them	☐	☐
Movements appear smooth	☐	☐
Walks backward	☐	☐
Skips	☐	☐
Right or left handedness is established	☐	☐
Uses glue correctly and easily	☐	☐

Figure 2–23 This child cuts with little difficulty.

Social/Personal Development

	Observed	Not Observed
Chooses own friends, may exclude a peer	☐	☐
Plays simple table games, plays competitive games (Figure 2–24)	☐	☐
Engages in group play, assigning roles, making decisions	☐	☐
Wants fair play	☐	☐
Interacts with peers and adults	☐	☐
Respects property and others	☐	☐
Leadership skills appear	☐	☐
Ability to follow peers	☐	☐
Shares, waits turn	☐	☐

Figure 2–24 Five-year-olds enjoy playing simple games.

	Observed	Not Observed

Cognitive/Language Development

	Observed	Not Observed
Uses complete, complex sentences to express ideas	☐	☐
Records ideas using drawing, letter-like forms, invented spelling	☐	☐
Recognizes letters and some words (Figure 2–25)	☐	☐
Recognizes numerals	☐	☐
Recognizes shapes	☐	☐
Understands patterns and sequencing	☐	☐
Understands one-to-one correspondence	☐	☐
Understands categories	☐	☐
Compares, arranges in order	☐	☐
Understands positional words	☐	☐
Understands rhyming words	☐	☐

Figure 2–25 Children's language development enables letter and word identification.

Emotional Development/Feelings

	Observed	Not Observed
Shows self-control (Figure 2–26)	☐	☐
Separates from parents	☐	☐
Comfortable with large groups	☐	☐
Cooperative attitude	☐	☐
Resolves conflicts verbally	☐	☐
Responds well to corrections or suggestions	☐	☐

Figure 2–26 This girl is showing self-control over her emotions.

DEVELOPMENTAL CHECKLIST
6–8-Year-Olds

	Observed	Not Observed

Physical Growth/Motor Development

	Observed	Not Observed
Rate of growth slows, but growth spurts occur	☐	☐
Enjoys team sports	☐	☐
Repeats skill for mastery (bike riding, skating, swimming, etc.)	☐	☐
Forms letters and numbers well (Figure 2–27)	☐	☐
Loss of teeth	☐	☐
Body develops more proportionately	☐	☐
Visual difficulties may surface	☐	☐
Shows coordination of large and small motor skills	☐	☐
Draws a person with clothes and body parts	☐	☐

Figure 2–27 By age eight, a child can write numbers and letters clearly.

Social/Personal Development

	Observed	Not Observed
Prefers own sex, less boy–girl interaction (Figure 2–28)	☐	☐
Forms peer groups	☐	☐
Works and plays independently	☐	☐
Takes responsibility	☐	☐
Wants to please	☐	☐
Enjoys imaginative play	☐	☐
Works well in a group or alone	☐	☐
Communicates well/engages in conversation	☐	☐
Develops self-control	☐	☐

Figure 2–28 Children between the ages of six and eight prefer same-sex interactions.

	Observed	Not Observed

Cognitive/Language Development

	Observed	Not Observed
Speaks in complex sentences	☐	☐
Solves problems	☐	☐
Can distinguish fantasy from reality	☐	☐
Uses hands-on manipulatives for understanding concepts	☐	☐
Longer attention span develops	☐	☐
Interested in more knowledge of the world	☐	☐
Differences in abilities begin to show	☐	☐
Conscious of others and compares work	☐	☐
Becoming an accomplished reader (Figure 2–29)	☐	☐

Figure 2–29 A child can read independently by age eight.

Emotional Development/Feelings

	Observed	Not Observed
Worries	☐	☐
May show outbursts of emotions (Figure 2–30)	☐	☐
Desires praise	☐	☐
Learning how to express feelings appropriately	☐	☐
Shows empathy	☐	☐
Sense of humor expands	☐	☐
Can be sensitive, has feelings hurt easily	☐	☐

Figure 2–30 Emotional outbursts are not uncommon from age six to eight.

ASSESSMENT METHOD 2:
Parent Interviews

$\mathcal{W}$hat can I do to assess young children?

The second method of assessment is through parent interviews.

Figure 2–31 Conducting parent interviews is an invaluable assessment tool.

Talk to parents or guardians about their child (Figure 2–31).

*W*hom should I interview?

Adults with the direct responsibilty of caring for the child should be interviewed.

Figure 2–32 Family structures have changed so that "parent interviews" may be conducted with grandparents or guardians.

Parents, grandparents, or guardians of the children in your classroom can be interviewed (Figure 2–32).

𝒲here will this activity take place?

This activity will occur at your school.

Figure 2–33 Teachers should hold parent interviews in a quiet place without the child present.

When interviewing parents and guardians

- find a quiet place where you can talk privately (Figure 2–33).
- talk to adults without the child.

*W*hen should I talk to the parents of my children?

Parents should be contacted two to four weeks after the first day, in the middle of the year, and at the end of the year (optional).

Remember to

■ plan the annual calendar with conference days pre-set if possible.

■ use a substitute teacher or volunteer so that you can schedule one or two full days to visit with parents.

■ depend on the director of your center for support in scheduling.

■ schedule 20- to 30-minute sessions per family.

■ include the portfolio containing the narrative summary, which should be given to the parent at the end of the year. You can make a decision to have another conference at that time if you feel it is necessary.

*H*ow will I conduct an interview?

Interviews should be conducted in an informative, but friendly, manner.

When conducting interviews

■ post a schedule for interviews (this time frame must be supported by your director).

■ *smile* as you greet the parents or guardians.

■ plan to say something positive about the child as you start the conference.

■ be enthusiastic and excited that you are teaching their child.

■ be warm, friendly, open, and eager to listen.

■ tell the parents that the interview is a way for you to discover more about their child.

■ make a copy of the interview forms on pages 47–50 (or Appendix B), or make up your own.

Why should I conduct parent interviews?

Parent interviews should be conducted to learn important information about each child.

During parent interviews

■ you will understand how parents see their child.

■ you will learn about the home life of the child.

■ parents reveal strengths, weaknesses, fears, and other facts that give you better insight into each child so that you can better plan activities children need and enjoy.

Teachers share their thoughts and experiences surrounding assessment methods used with children of various age levels.

Kindergartners

> 66 I conducted my first interview about four weeks into the school year. I was shocked at how much I learned! I have taught for 10 years, but this was my first experience using parent interviews. It gave me more insight into how parents view their own children. 99

> 66 I was only able to do this because of support from our director. I used two full days to schedule parents, allowing 30 minutes for each interview. She hired a substitute teacher for my classroom. 99

> 66 It is the most valuable form of assessment I have used in my years of teaching. It allowed me to get to know the parents; therefore, helped me have a much better understanding of their child. When the two days ended, I saw the children in a different way. 99

4-year-olds

> 66 I interviewed my parents this year and it was extremely helpful to learn more about the home life of each child. I could immediately see why children acted like they did or talked like they did after I interviewed their parents. Next year I will schedule two visits, one early in the year and one in the spring. I think the visit early in the year is the most critical. I found myself to be more patient and understanding of certain children after the interviews. 99

PARENT INTERVIEW FORM

Beginning of the Year

Child _____ Date _____

Parent/guardian_____

To begin the conference, say the following:

Thank you for trusting me with your child this year. I know it is going to be a great year. I have already noticed that _____ loves the pets in our classroom. He must really be an animal lover.

Parents will respond because you have opened the conversation in a positive, friendly way. You may begin with questions similar to those that follow or make up your own.

1. Tell me about your family. (Who lives in the house, how many brothers or sisters, etc.?)

2. What kinds of things do you do as a family? What things are you interested in? (Sports, music, animals, etc.) How do you spend free time as a family?

3. Do both parents work? What kinds of jobs do you have? What hours do you work?

4. What is the most important thing I need to know about your child?

5. Tell me about his/her eating and sleeping habits.

6. How do you discipline at home?

7. Could you offer some strengths and weaknesses that you see in your child?

8. Do you see your child as
   - a leader or a follower?
   - independent or dependent?
   - a contented child or an unhappy child?
   - shy or confident?
   - having self-control or lacking self-control?

At this point, you can share some strengths or positives that you have noticed. You also can state the immediate goals you have set for the child, for example:
   - learning to follow two-step directions
   - strengthening fine motor skills
   - striving to be less argumentative during outdoor play

To close the conference, say the following:

I would like to share some things that we will be doing in class this year because I want you to feel that you are a part of your child's activities.

At this time, have some special things ready to share about you and your classroom.

Please feel welcome to visit often. There will be notes posted outside the door (or sent home). I will communicate often to let you know how _____ is doing. Please send me notes or call when there is something that I need to know as well. It is going to be a good year. I am so glad you could come and visit me today. You have a precious child and I look forward to being a part of your family this year.

PARENT INTERVIEW FORM

Middle of the Year

Child _____ Date _____

Parent/guardian_____

Open the conference with a positive comment.

You know the child well, so you should have several positive things to say. Write them down.

- Have some specific items from the portfolio to share with the parents. It could be photographs, artwork, scribbling or writing samples, an audiocassette tape of their child's language development, a checklist of things he/she can do, anecdotal records, etc. Discuss each item. This is the opening for discussing problem areas as well as strengths.

- Explain that you will save these items in the portfolio, but they will be given to the parents at the end of the year. You can offer the parent a copy of the checklist if you choose to use it.

- Have a list of positive things to say about that child.

- Discuss any problems after the positive things have been mentioned. Be sure not to label the child.

- This is the time to address any problems or issues. You need to mention that the year is one-half over and specific problems may need their advice, help, and direction. You have had the child long enough to have documentation on any major issue and written documentation will be critical as you discuss, *not label*, problems. This is a good time to decide together the progress of those problem areas.

- The director of your center can be part of the conference if you feel more confident having someone of authority with you.

- End the conference on a positive comment.

Thank the parents for coming and for caring.

Conference Suggestions:

What documentation will you show?

Child's strengths:

Child's weaknesses (set goals today):

Ask for any parental concerns not discussed before today.

Teacher and parent goals for the remainder of the year:

ASSESSMENT METHOD 3:
Self-Portraits

*W*hat can I do to assess young children?

The third method of assessment involves observation of self-portraits.

Figure 2–34 Children can begin drawing self-portraits by age three.

Ask children to draw themselves.

Who can draw self-portraits?

Most children from age three to eight can draw self-portraits.

Figure 2–35 Children feel encouraged to draw when a creative space is provided with supplies such as crayons, markers, and paper.

When considering self-portraits as an assessment tool, remember

- children who can hold a pencil, crayon, or marker can attempt to draw themselves (Figure 2–35).
- younger children may draw with more detail than older children.
- some children may only scribble.
- to be very accepting of any effort.

*W*here will this activity take place?

Drawing self-portraits will occur in your classroom during center time.

This is a great activity for the art center!

*W*hen should my children draw pictures of themselves?

Children should be encouraged to draw themselves so developmental growth can be assessed (Figure 2–36).

Figure 2–36 Many developmental changes can be observed by having children draw themselves at different points throughout the year.

Self-portraits should be drawn at three times during the year, in the

■ fall.

■ winter.

■ spring.

*H*ow will I organize this activity?

Set up the art center for a week and provide materials such as paper, crayons, markers, and pencils.

Figure 2–37 Each child's portrait should include their name, date, and age at the time.

In the art center

■ encourage all students to draw themselves (Figure 2–37) and write their name (if they can write).

■ write the child's name and date on each portrait.

Why should my students draw self-portraits?

The child's ability to make a person gives insight to the child's overall capability.

Some points to remember about self-portraits.

■ A self-portrait shows development in body awareness and of fine motor skills. Body awareness shows that the child has perceptual awareness.

■ The human figure consists of all the boundaries contained in letter shapes.

■ Children's art reflects their thinking and knowledge of their world. As children grow and understand more about the world, they gain new concepts, and their drawings change by becoming more like real-world objects. The detail of their drawings increases as their knowledge of the world increases.

■ The idea that a child's picture may be related to how they are functioning intellectually was studied by a researcher, Florence Laura Goodenough (1975). She collected children's drawings of a person and studied these drawings. Her work showed that the detail and realism of the human body increased as a child's knowledge increased. She believed that a child's drawing of any object reflected their concept of that object.

Teachers share their thoughts and experiences surrounding assessment methods used with children of various age levels.

Kindergartners

    ❝It was always so exciting in September to see how well my children could draw themselves. I couldn't wait to see the results, because I felt I had a better understanding of my class as a whole when I looked at the details, or even lack of details. I loved seeing the growth in January, and again in May. I could tell the children were learning.❞

Pre-kindergartners

    ❝It was so satisfying to display the three self-portraits at the end of the year. It gave me such insight to each child, and the parents could see the growth as well. Of course, some children's portraits showed more changes over time than others.❞

3-year-olds

    ❝I only started this practice in my class last year. When we compared portraits of three-, four-, and five-year-olds, the other teachers were surprised that many of my three-year-olds had much more detail than the older children.❞

4-year-olds

    ❝Pictures often say more than words and I found this to be true with this one assessment tool.❞

Samples of Self-Portraits

Three self-portraits of one child follow. They show development at three times during the four-year-old year in preschool. The child drew the first picture at 4 years, 10 months (Figure 2–38a), the second at 5 years, 2 months (Figure 2–38b), and the third at 5 years, 6 months (Figure 2–38c).

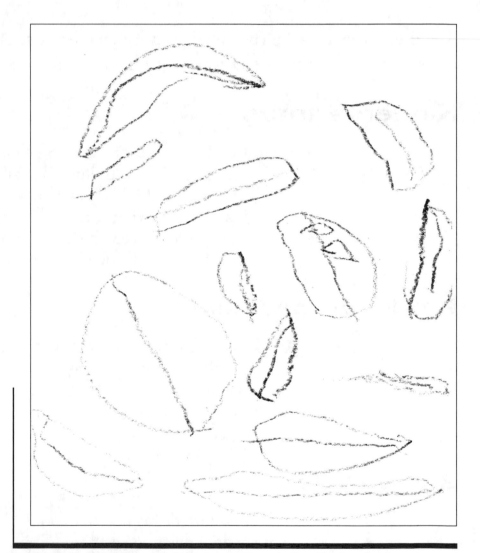

Figure 2–38a At four years, ten months, Zachary's closed shapes show that his fine motor skills are progressing along with his mental processes.

Figure 2–38b At five years, two months, Zachary now illustrates that he understands more about a person's shape. Children draw a head first; the body comes a little later.

Figure 2–38c At five years, six months, Zachary illustrates a more advanced concept of a human body. He now has a nose, mouth, and body.

ASSESSMENT METHOD 4:
Scribbling, Drawing, and Writing Samples

*W*hat can I do to assess young children?

The fourth method of assessment uses work samples from the children.

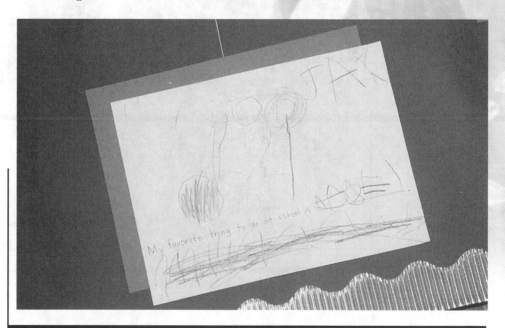

Figure 2–39 This child's sample demonstrates scribbling, drawing, and writing (through inventive spelling).

Save work samples from each child (Figure 2–39).

Who can scribble, draw, and write?

Any child who can hold a crayon or pencil and is given the opportunity, can write, draw, or scribble.

Figure 2–40 Children enjoy writing and drawing and are proud of their accomplishments.

All children enjoy scribbling, drawing, and writing (Figure 2–40). They love to see their work on paper.

Where will this activity take place?

Children will scribble, draw, and write any place—indoors or outdoors.

When using this assessment method

■ your classroom should be a place that encourages scribbling, drawing, and writing.

■ you can have a writing or drawing center that is always open.

■ tools for scribbling, drawing, and writing should always be available under your supervision.

$\mathcal{W}$hen should I save scribbling, drawing, and writing samples?

Save at least one work sample per month for each child.

Work samples can be in a variety of forms.

■ Label each sample with the child's name and date.

■ You can save as many samples as you would like. This choice may depend on your space and storage method.

$\mathcal{H}$ow can I encourage scribbling, drawing, and writing?

Set up a permanent area to encourage scribbling, drawing, and writing (Figure 2–41).

Figure 2–41 Art and writing centers help encourage children to participate often.

Encourage these activities by

■ providing materials such as paper, crayons, markers, and pencils.

■ allowing all students to feel free to draw and write often.

■ writing the child's name and date on the sample you want to save.

■ making positive comments about any effort.

*W*hy should I save writings, drawings, and scribblings of each child?

These samples provide evidence of typical, everyday performance, providing rich documentation of the child's learning.

There are many positive reasons to save each child's work.

■ Parents find work samples, saved over time, to be helpful in understanding stages of growth and development.

■ Work samples over time show the child's progress in developing fine motor skills as they move from large scribbles across the page to closed circles.

■ Children can see their own growth as their writings and drawings change over time.

Teachers share their thoughts and experiences surrounding assessment methods used with children of various age levels.

3-year-olds

❝It was amazing to compare scribbling samples from September to December. After just four months, many children had learned to draw circles. It was so easy to show parents the change. In May, there were actually many recognizable shapes, not just scribbles. I can tell a parent that a child is learning, but it is so much more meaningful to have evidence that shows the learning.❞

4-year-olds

❝Keeping scribbles and drawings all through the year helped me see the growth in my four-year-olds. I stored them in each child's file folder, which worked well for me. But, I wanted an easy way to keep track of students and what I had saved, so I created an alphabetized list of my students, then copied it many times. I kept one list handy each week so I could check off each name when I had kept the sample for documentation in their portfolio. I would write a category at the top of the list of what I was saving. For example, I might be saving documentation of fine motor development, so I collected cutting samples from each child.❞

Scribbling Samples

The following samples show the growth and development of a child as his scribbling moved from lines (Figure 2–42a) to closed figures (Figure 2–42b) over a six month period. A parent or teacher does not have to take a college class to observe the change in the drawings. By observation alone, it is apparent that the child has developed stronger fine motor skills with the ability to form closed shapes, not just lines. Parents enjoy seeing the changes over time, and they know this is a product that indicates growth.

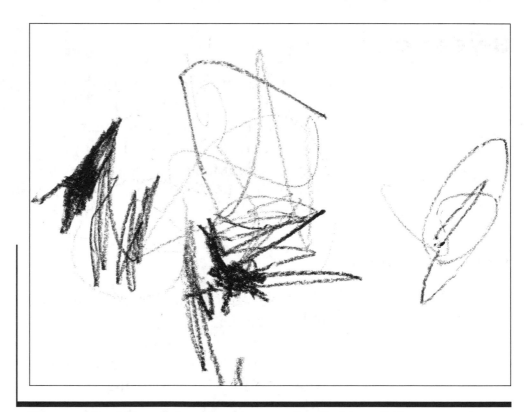

Figure 2–42a At two years, ten months, Cody's scribbles are random and just beginning to show closed shapes. (October, 1999)

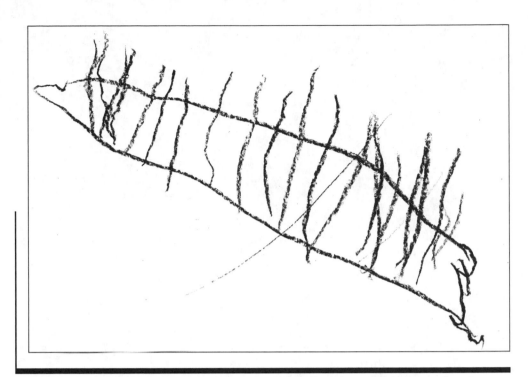

Figure 2–42b Just seven months later, Cody's scribbles are showing definite shapes, symmetry, and controlled lines. (May, 2000)

ASSESSMENT METHOD 5: Audio (or Video) Tapes

*W*hat can I do to assess young children?

The fifth method of assessment uses audio and video tapes to record a child's development.

Figure 2–43 Recorded audio tapes can show tremendous growth in a child's language development over time.

Record each child talking (language development) on tape (Figure 2–43).

*W*hom should I record?

All children can be recorded.

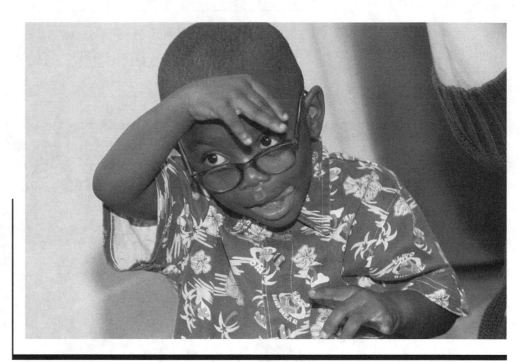

Figure 2–44 Not all children will be this comfortable talking in front of a video camera or on an audio tape.

Children of all ages make sounds or words.

■ Some children may talk more than others (Figure 2–44).

■ Some children may be understood easier than others.

■ Be very encouraging and accepting of children learning to talk.

*W*here will this activity take place?

This assessment method can be performed anywhere you and the child feel comfortable.

Audio or video taping can be done
- ■ in your classroom.
- ■ in the library.
- ■ indoors or outdoors.

*W*hen will this activity take place?

Taping can take place anytime you have time to listen to or view one child.

Figure 2–45 Children can often be observed talking to themselves while playing independently.

Audio or video taping can be part of your weekly routine

■ during center time (Figure 2–45).

■ during library period.

■ during show and tell.

■ when volunteers are available to work with the class.

*H*ow do I record my children on tape?

Record the child talking to another child, retelling a story, or sharing a show-and-tell object.

Audio taping young children can be fun.

■ Ask each parent to provide one audio cassette.

■ Use a blank label on each tape so that you can add the child's name and the dates of the recording sessions.

■ Keep a tape player in your classroom.

■ Students love to hear a tape recording of themselves.

Why should I make recordings of my children using audio tapes?

This assessment method provides good documentation of speech and language development over time.

Recordings can be helpful because

■ if the child has a speech or language problem, a tape will be helpful documentation to parents.

■ children love to listen to themselves and hear their own growth and development of language.

■ the tape can reveal the child's thought processes.

■ a tape is objective.

■ a taped interview with a child can document the child's ability to focus for a reasonable amount of time.

Teachers share their thoughts and experiences surrounding assessment methods used with children of various age levels.

Kindergartners

"What a wonderful way to document language development! I found this one assessment method to be time-consuming, but very worthwhile. You need to decide early in the year if you have enough help in the classroom to make tapes. I was fortunate to have college students working daily in my room. They would ask the children to retell stories, but some students actually conducted short interviews with my children.

The children loved hearing themselves on tape. The differences from September to May were incredible. The sophistication of speech patterns was obvious, but I would never have realized it without the recordings.

The one thing I like the most about this method is that it is purely objective. I didn't have to make judgments; I just let the parents hear the speech and language for themselves."

3-year-olds

"I used audio tapes for the first time this year. I was surprised at the growth and change in language after just three months. The sentences were longer and the vocabulary was much larger. It did take time to tape the children, but it was extremely valuable in looking at language development."

ASSESSMENT METHOD 6:
Anecdotal Records

What can I do to assess young children?

The last method of assessment documents children's development through the use of anecdotal records.

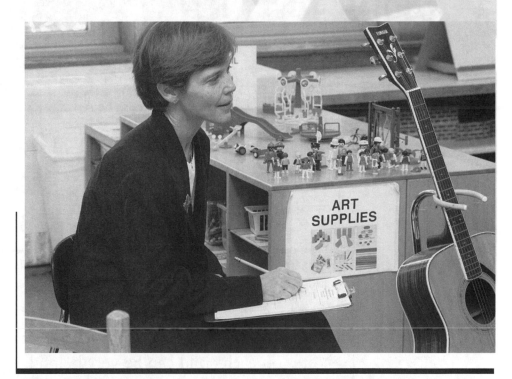

Figure 2–46 Anecdotal records provide a quick, immediate process for recording observations.

Anecdotal records (notes) work well alone or with other assessment methods such as documentation for checklists and parent interviews.

*W*hom should I make anecdotal records of?

Children of all ages should be observed for anecdotal records.

Figure 2–47 An anecdotal record on this child could note that she used facial expressions to convey her displeasure at the activity.

Notes on each child can be very helpful.

■ Take short notes describing events that happen to the children in your classroom.

■ Choose a child and record specific examples to show social skills, feelings, physical development, or language skills (Figure 2–47).

■ The director of the school can also make notes or comments on a child.

■ You must be sure to keep anecdotal records on *all* children.

*W*here will I take notes, or anecdotes?

Any place you are observing the children is appropriate for taking notes.

Figure 2–48 Any time or place children are observed is a good opportunity to take anecdotes.

Note-taking can take place

■ in centers.

■ outdoors at playtime.

■ in the lunch or snack area.

■ in the classroom during naptime.

■ anywhere (Figure 2–48).

When should I take anecdotal records?

Schedule only a few times each day to take anecdotal records, so it is not an overwhelming task.

Good planning makes this assessment method very useful.

■ Once a week, make a note on each child. This is approximately four times per month, giving a great overview of the child's progress. If you have 15 children, make three notes each day.

■ Decide on the time of day to record notes on each child. You may want to observe a child's progress in social interactions, so you will record notes during outdoor play or in centers. If you are concerned about a child's eating habits, you may choose lunch or snack time.

*H*ow will I take these anecdotal records?

Record a few sentences that describe what is happening. Include the child's behaviors, reactions, and comments.

Once you have decided at which learning time during the day you plan to observe

- ■ use 3″ x 5″ sticky notes and a fine point pen.

- ■ write the child's name and date, very small, on the top of the sticky note.

- ■ keep several sticky notes on a clipboard; one for each child you are observing that day.

- ■ record facts, not opinions.

- ■ make notes of strengths, not just weaknesses. It is a good practice to record what they *can* do, not just what they *cannot* do.

- ■ be specific, using the child's words when appropriate.

(See Appendix C for a sample anecdote.)

Why should I keep anecdotal records?

Anecdotal records provide a systematic way
of tracking how and what students are learning.

These notes have many uses.

■ When you keep these notes over an entire year, they provide an objective picture of how that child has grown and changed. They are easy to share with parents.

■ These notes allow you to collect information continuously so that you can identify the strengths and weaknesses of each child over time. You can use this information to plan your daily activities, as you reflect on what students need to know.

■ This is a great way to determine if a child has mastered a specific skill listed on the developmental checklist.

Teachers share their thoughts and experiences surrounding assessment methods used with children of various ages.

18-months–2 ½-year-olds

" I tried keeping anecdotal records this year for the first time. I used the small yellow sticky notes to write down things that I thought were important. I posted a chart that was divided into squares, one square for each child's name. I could easily see if I had not made notes on a child. This method of note-taking helped me communicate with my children's parents. It works well for me. "

3-year-olds

" I discovered that the best way to accurately mark the developmental checklist was to write short notes. I took most of my notes when children were playing outside. It was a good place to document physical growth as well as social interactions. "

Kindergartners

" I kept anecdotal records because I was trying new assessment methods for the portfolios of my kindergarten students this year. I particularly liked this one because I had so many children with special needs. The notes gave me important documentation for specific problems. I talked with parents often, and the written observations kept me more objective. "

Summary

This section of the book was designed so that a teacher can quickly pull and use the method (or methods) that best fits the particular classroom. It will be rare for a teacher to use all six in one year because of time constraints.

During the study at the Early Childhood Development Center at Lamar University, I asked teachers to read all of the assessment techniques, choose the ones that most fit their style, and then implement the plan for one year. What I experienced and observed during that year was revealing.

- Most teachers did not have an existing assessment plan and were delighted when they saw the results over time.
- Each time I entered the center, teachers could not say enough about their observations and what they had learned about the children.
- I also found that each teacher had a different opinion on the amount of time they wanted to invest and which methods were most appealing to them.

After reflecting on my own experiences and from observing teachers for one year, the most important advice I can give is to *find a way to assess growth and development of the children you teach*. The methods presented here can be used alone or in combination with the other methods. Remember that the developmental checklist should only serve as broad guidelines or goals for your children over the course of one year. Read the other five methods, to decide which might provide the best documentation for those broad goals.

Assessment of children should not take over your life and totally consume you as a teacher. If you choose a method you like, embrace it, and enjoy implementing it. It is important to find a good fit between you, your children, and your assessment techniques. You will feel much better about yourself and your classroom if you take time to assess, and then share the documentation you have collected. Parents will be appreciative, the child will benefit, and your overall program will become more child-centered.

PART 3

Pulling It All Together

Now What?

In Part 2, you were introduced to six methods used to assess students. That creates a whole new set of questions! Is one method better than another? How many types of assessment do I really need? Is one enough? What do I do with all of the materials I have saved on each child? Will assessment help me identify children with problems? How does it really help me teach and plan?

All of these questions are valid and must be answered for the assessment process to have meaning. In Part 3, an attempt is made to answer these questions and help teachers get on the road to assessment with ease.

Pulling it All Together—
A Final Narrative Summary

You have now saved lots of good materials, but what do you do with them? (Ideas for storage will be given later.) What does it all mean? What does it really show about the child?

You can use the information and work you have saved to not only document achievement of developmental milestones, but to create a final product for both the parents and the child's next teacher. Many teachers pull the information together in a *narrative summary* at the end of the year (Figure 3–1). That simply means that you will write a few paragraphs to

Figure 3–1 A narrative summary documents the child's overall growth and development throughout the year.

summarize the growth and development of each student. This written product can be the final piece added to the portfolio and given to the parents. The Lamar Early Childhood Development Center makes a copy of this summary and keeps it in a file folder as documentation on each child.

It is a great idea to write a narrative summary that documents the four broad developmental areas. It will be easy for a parent to follow if you separate your comments into a social, emotional, cognitive, and physical development format. You can discuss the child's progress in each area, using the information saved in the portfolio as documentation for your comments. It is important to be as positive as possible, giving examples of what the child can do, focusing on strengths. A sample of a paragraph from a narrative summary follows:

> **Physical Growth/Motor Development:** Joseph is now holding a pencil correctly and often chooses to write or draw during center time. He cuts well and often helps others who have trouble cutting on the line. He is developing his large muscles in our outdoor play area by riding tricycles, climbing, and playing with the large balls. He has mastered catching the large ball after one bounce. He wants to skip and is working hard to learn.

This paragraph is easy to write, taking only a few minutes, yet gives the parent and child's next year teacher a glimpse at what the child can do physically. It shows he is developing, growing, and learning (Figure 3–2). An example of the entire narrative summary is in Appendix D.

Figure 3–2 This boy is demonstrating his motor skill development by catching the ball as it is tossed.

How Many Types of Assessment Should I Use?

It will be your personal choice as to the number of assessment methods you choose. If you have not used assessment tools in the past, you should choose one that seems appropriate for your classroom setting.

Developmental Checklists

A good choice for a beginning teacher is the developmental checklist, as it helps you and your students' parents identify the milestones for that particular age. It is quick and easy to check, but be sure to refer to it several times during the year. It will help you become observant of details in each developmental area.

If you understand the four broad developmental areas from the checklists, you will see how your classroom activities connect, and encourage growth in those areas. The developmental checklist will also help parents understand the areas where their children are learning and growing.

Scribbling, Drawing, and Writing Samples

Saving work samples takes little time and effort. Any teacher can have success with this approach. The work samples document mastery of the skills listed on the developmental checklist, giving you products to show parents that illustrate growth and development (Figure 3–3).

Figure 3–3 Saving children's artwork in a portfolio provides a quick visual for parents of their children's development.

Anecdotal Records

Anecdotal recordkeeping is also one of the simplest methods to understand and implement. Keep notes and use them—along with the developmental checklist—to help parents understand how their child is growing. Your notes during the year can document the child's progress in the four key developmental areas: Physical Growth/Motor Development, Social/ Personal Development, Emotional Development/Feelings, and Cognitive/ Language Development.

Use any or all of these three easy assessment methods until you are comfortable adding others. The more documentation you keep, the better overall picture you will have of the "whole child". It is up to you to choose the methods that best suit you and your classroom setting. It is critical that you feel comfortable with the method, and that you find a way to assess your students on a consistent basis.

Portfolios as a Way to Save Student Work

The manner in which you save developmental checklists and other evaluation products is an important decision you need to make at the beginning of the school year. A **portfolio** is one method used by many teachers to save information. There is much written today about the use of portfolios for assessment purposes, but what exactly is a portfolio?

Shores and Grace (1998, p. 39) define the portfolio as "a collection of items that reveal different aspects of an individual child's growth and development over time". Therefore, you can think of a portfolio as simply a container filled with items you want to save on each child. Each child needs a separate container or portfolio.

The Working Portfolio

For years, my college students created **working portfolios** (Figure 3–4). They collected information during their junior and senior years of fieldwork and student teaching, only completing a final **professional portfolio** at the time of graduation. The items they saved documented a mastery of the state objectives for teaching and learning. I loved that term, "working portfolio," as it implied an *ongoing process*, not a *final product*.

I also think of assessment for children as an ongoing process; therefore, the term working portfolio can apply to teachers of young children as well. There are many different kinds of portfolios, but the one described here is a working portfolio used to store the products from assessment. It should be a portfolio where information is constantly being collected and added over time.

What Does a Working Portfolio Look Like?

You have many choices of how to actually create a portfolio for each child. Your decision should be a practical one and it takes thought and planning.

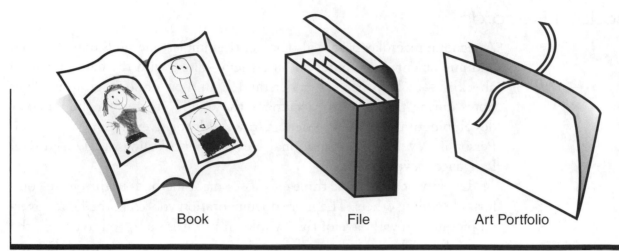

Book   File   Art Portfolio

Figure 3–4   A working portfolio can be a book, an accordion file, a shoebox, or an art portfolio.

Many teachers experiment, trying a new method each year. Some storage units (portfolios) that have worked in the past include shoeboxes, file folders, commercially bought accordion folders, and homemade paper folders (Figure 3–4). You must feel comfortable with the method you choose, but one consideration in this choice should be storage space. If you use a shoebox, you must have a place for *lots* of shoeboxes! Storage space may dictate what you decide to use.

Teacher-Made Portfolios

The **teacher-made portfolio**, made from poster board or tag board, is one that I have seen used effectively (Figure 3–5). It is sturdy, easy to make, and works like a large file folder.

To make a working portfolio from tag board, follow these directions.

1. Fold one piece of poster board in half.
2. Fold one side down about five inches and staple the sides together.
3. This fold creates a place (on the back at the top) for the name so that it is easy to see, similar to a real file folder.

This portfolio is large and sturdy. It will not only store big projects and artwork, but will provide space to store all the assessment methods described in this book. This folder is easy to use and is durable for an entire school year.

A large banana box (from the produce section of the grocery store) works as a great file box, where these large, teacher-made, working portfolios can be stored in alphabetical order.

Children with Special Needs and Portfolios

It is not your job as teacher to "label" children. Most teachers are not qualified or trained to give labels and must leave that to pediatricians,

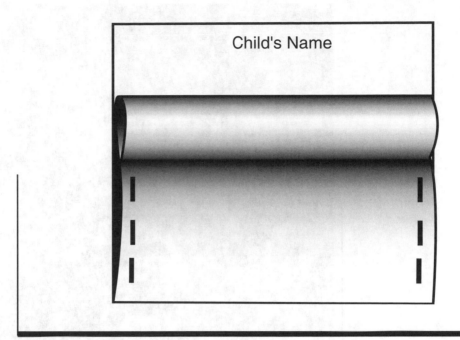

Figure 3–5 A teacher-made portfolio is simple and cost-effective.

psychologists, psychiatrists, or other trained specialists. However, it is your job as a teacher to be aware of "red flags" that can signal problems. For some children with special needs, early intervention is best. But, in other instances, growth and maturity over time are the only things needed to correct the areas of concern. Professionals can help parents and teachers make the decisions regarding these questions. If you understand the four broad development areas including the basic developmental milestones for each area, it will be easier to spot the "red flags."

Assessment from documentation described in this book can be mostly objective. Many times, the objective assessment tools will show that a child is not progressing in one or more areas. Parents will be able to see the growth and development or *lack* of growth and development if you use authentic assessment methods such as the portfolio approach explained earlier. With this documentation, a professional can be consulted if parents and teachers together see areas of concern.

How Will This Portfolio Approach Help Me Teach?

The National Association for the Education of Young Children (NAEYC) is an organization that publishes standards for assessment. The standards state that assessment of children must be used to benefit the child. When you look at what children can or cannot do (based on your evalutions), you make decisions on what you need to teach (Bredekamp & Copple, 1997).

By understanding the broad developmental milestones for the age of children you teach, you can plan daily activities to help children achieve those skills. Even though milestones are not daily teaching objectives, they

Figure 3–6 Developmental milestones help teachers assess this boy's motor development.

can serve as an overall guide for what children need to know and be able to do at a certain age (Figure 3–6). You must be certain your teaching activities are helping your children achieve those milestones.

For example: If you want two-year-olds to learn to climb, jump, and hop, plan activities that include many opportunities for children to play and participate in those kinds of things. To assess a child's ability in that area, observe the child completing the activity. You can document a child's success during this observation with a quick notation (anecdotal record) at outside playtime. If you observe a child who cannot successfully climb, jump, and hop, then it is your job as the teacher to plan more activities and work with that child on those skills. This is using *assessment to drive instruction.* You will be encouraging and teaching the things that children need to know and be able to do.

The Checklist Is Not a Curriculum

Developmental milestones, as listed in this book, provide a baseline understanding for the skills children usually have at a particular age. The director or principal should provide more detailed teaching goals for the children in your center or school. There may also be state guidelines or objectives that must be met. You will find that your teaching objectives will fall under the basic skills listed in the developmental checklists provided. Remember that the checklist is only a baseline for assessment of growth and development, not an entire curriculum for teaching and learning.

Summary

Assessment is time-consuming, but worthwhile. The knowledge gained will help you understand each child and know what you need to teach. As a teacher, you must try different strategies and find those that fit your own classroom environment. Practicing the techniques from this book will help you understand the "total child" and all areas of development. These methods provide specific information to share with parents, and can be used to provide an overall picture of the child.

Appendix A

Developmental Checklists

Understanding Developmental Checklists

- The developmental milestones listed in the sample developmental checklists that follow are broad skills intended to give an overall picture of children in specific age groups.

- You will discover that some skills belong in more than one area of development.

- Children grow and change rapidly from birth to age eight. Become familiar with the broad developmental milestones, understanding that all children develop at different rates.

- Do not use the checklist as a report card of strengths and weaknesses, but as a guide for normal development.

- The checklist can be a discussion tool for development by making notes or comments about specific characteristics. This is helpful when talking to parents.

- Use the checklist as you make anecdotal records. It will serve as a guide for the four broad areas of development.

- You can add or delete skills. There is an endless list of characteristics and skills for each age group. You decide how detailed you want your list.

DEVELOPMENTAL CHECKLIST
0–12 Months

	Observed	Not Observed
Physical Growth/Motor Development		
Looks around (2 months)	☐	☐
Laughs aloud (3–5 months)	☐	☐
Controls head movements (about 4 months)	☐	☐
Notices hands/feet and plays with them (3–5 months)	☐	☐
Rolls over (4–6 months)	☐	☐
Sits up without support (6–8 months)	☐	☐
Holds bottle (6–8 months)	☐	☐
Crawls (6–8 months)	☐	☐
Walks with support	☐	☐
Imitates adults' facial gestures	☐	☐
Reaches, grasps	☐	☐
Puts objects in mouth	☐	☐
Picks things up with thumb and finger	☐	☐
Picks up toys that are dropped	☐	☐
Teeth appear (6–12 months)	☐	☐
Social/Personal Development		
Smiles spontaneously (0–3 months)	☐	☐
Recognizes mother	☐	☐
Begins to notice strangers	☐	☐
Enjoys personal play and contact	☐	☐
Vocalizes, squeals with joy	☐	☐
Imitates actions	☐	☐
Participates in "peek-a-boo" and other games	☐	☐
May cry when left alone	☐	☐
Cognitive/Language Development		
Responds to different sounds/voices	☐	☐
Studies and inspects things for long periods of time	☐	☐
Notices if you hide an object	☐	☐
Becomes curious	☐	☐

	Observed	Not Observed
Cognitive/Language Development (*continued*)		
Learns and responds to "no"	☐	☐
Follows object with eyes	☐	☐
Imitates others	☐	☐
Puts objects in and out of containers	☐	☐
Emotional Development/Feelings		
Smiles	☐	☐
Squeals with joy and pleasure	☐	☐
Cries differently for hunger, pain, cold, wet	☐	☐
Shows fear by using body movements	☐	☐
Shows affection	☐	☐
Begins to show anger (9–14 months)	☐	☐

DEVELOPMENTAL CHECKLIST
12–24 Months

	Observed	Not Observed
Physical Growth/Motor Development		
Teething continues	☐	☐
Crawls well, stands alone well	☐	☐
Walks without help	☐	☐
Pushes, pulls toys	☐	☐
Sits in chair	☐	☐
Moves to music	☐	☐
Throws, kicks a ball	☐	☐
Crawls down stairs backward	☐	☐
Stacks blocks	☐	☐
Uses a spoon, chews food	☐	☐
Turns book pages	☐	☐
Jumps up and down	☐	☐
Holds glass	☐	☐
Opens doors and cabinets	☐	☐
Scribbles, paints with whole arm	☐	☐
Starts elimination control	☐	☐
Social/Personal Development		
Recognizes self in mirror	☐	☐
Understands own name and responds	☐	☐
Initiates play	☐	☐
Imitates adults	☐	☐
Helps pick up toys	☐	☐
Identifies body parts	☐	☐
Shows interest in playing with peers, enjoys others	☐	☐
Becomes possessive	☐	☐
Cognitive/Language Development		
Talks, words accompany gestures	☐	☐
Responds to simple directions	☐	☐
Begins to put words together	☐	☐
Enjoys rhythm and rhyme	☐	☐

	Observed	Not Observed

Cognitive/Language Development (continued)

	Observed	Not Observed
Likes to hear same story over again	☐	☐
Takes apart and puts back together	☐	☐
Looks for hidden objects	☐	☐
Shows signs of memory development	☐	☐
Solves problems through trial and error	☐	☐

Emotional Development/Feelings

	Observed	Not Observed
Begins to show shame, guilt, shyness	☐	☐
Shows frustrations	☐	☐
May show moods	☐	☐
May rebel, resist, runs away	☐	☐
Humor develops	☐	☐
Can be negative, says no	☐	☐
Laughs, shows joys	☐	☐

DEVELOPMENTAL CHECKLIST
24–36 Months

	Observed	Not Observed

Physical Growth/Motor Development

	Observed	Not Observed
Uses a spoon without spilling	☐	☐
Opens doors	☐	☐
Puts on coat	☐	☐
Washes and dries hands	☐	☐
Begins to cut with scissors	☐	☐
Uses one hand consistently	☐	☐
Runs forward, jumps in place, climbs	☐	☐
Stands on one foot	☐	☐
Walks on tiptoes	☐	☐
Kicks ball forward	☐	☐
Rides a tricycle	☐	☐
Marches to music	☐	☐

Social/Personal Development

	Observed	Not Observed
Uses words for wants and seeks teacher attention	☐	☐
Plays near others, then begins to play with others (in groups of 2 or 3 children)	☐	☐
Watches other children	☐	☐
Participates in group activities	☐	☐
Understands gender identity	☐	☐
Helpful	☐	☐
Shows independence	☐	☐
May have imaginary playmates	☐	☐

Cognitive/Language Development

	Observed	Not Observed
Uses words to express wants, makes sentences, answers yes/no questions	☐	☐
Begins counting	☐	☐
Responds and follows directions	☐	☐
Matches similar objects	☐	☐
Enjoys books	☐	☐
Recognizes differences in you and me	☐	☐

	Observed	Not Observed

Cognitive/Language Development (continued)

	Observed	Not Observed
Gaining attention span	☐	☐
Explores world, very curious, asks questions	☐	☐
Can tell you what he/she is doing	☐	☐
Stacks rings according to size, attempts 2- and 3-piece puzzles	☐	☐
Gives first and last name	☐	☐
Asks "what" and "where" questions	☐	☐
Shows interest in toilet training	☐	☐

Emotional Development/Feelings

	Observed	Not Observed
May show fears	☐	☐
Intentional lying may begin (closer to age three)	☐	☐
Shows pride	☐	☐
Uses words for emotions, shows sympathy and affection	☐	☐
Feelings can be hurt	☐	☐
Associates facial expressions with emotions	☐	☐
Shows temper	☐	☐

DEVELOPMENTAL CHECKLIST
3-Year-Olds

	Observed	Not Observed
Physical Growth/Motor Development		
Copies circles	☐	☐
Manipulates clay, puzzles, scissors	☐	☐
Builds	☐	☐
Runs around obstacles	☐	☐
Walks on a line	☐	☐
Hops/balances on one foot	☐	☐
Steers and pedals tricycle	☐	☐
Throws ball overhand	☐	☐
Jumps with two feet	☐	☐
Begins to use zippers, buttons to dress	☐	☐
Social/Personal Development		
Tells name	☐	☐
May continue to play alongside others or join in the play	☐	☐
Shares, takes turns (may have difficulty with this)	☐	☐
Identifies others	☐	☐
Sings	☐	☐
Accepts responsibility/demonstrates self-control	☐	☐
Begins dramatic play/pretends	☐	☐
Cognitive/Language Development		
Solves problems	☐	☐
Listens attentively	☐	☐
Follows simple directions	☐	☐
Completes task	☐	☐
Can express self verbally	☐	☐
Compares size	☐	☐
Counts	☐	☐
Recognizes and matches colors	☐	☐
Draws picture, can explain it to an adult	☐	☐

	Observed	Not Observed

Cognitive/Language Development (continued)

	Observed	Not Observed
Asks "why" questions	☐	☐
Knows name, age	☐	☐
Has short attention span	☐	☐
Can group objects	☐	☐
Talks in sentences	☐	☐
Begins to understand time concepts	☐	☐
Refers to self as "I" or "me"	☐	☐
Speech is understandable, using sentences	☐	☐

Emotional Development/Feelings

	Observed	Not Observed
Is developing self-confidence	☐	☐
Expresses feelings in an appropriate manner	☐	☐
Accepts constructive criticism	☐	☐
Developing humor, may be silly	☐	☐
Can revert to toddler behavior of sucking thumb, crying, etc., if unhappy	☐	☐

DEVELOPMENTAL CHECKLIST
4-Year-Olds

	Observed	Not Observed
Physical Growth/Motor Development		
Draws, paints, uses scissors	☐	☐
Dresses and undresses without assistance	☐	☐
Walks stairs alone, alternating feet	☐	☐
Self-reliant in bathroom	☐	☐
Kicks, throws, bounces, catches a ball	☐	☐
Runs, hops, skips, jumps, gallops	☐	☐
Developing eye-hand coordination	☐	☐
Social/Personal Development		
Plays and interacts with others	☐	☐
Dramatic play is close to reality, using detail	☐	☐
Shows interest in gender differences	☐	☐
Tries new things	☐	☐
Participates/functions well in group activities	☐	☐
Works and plays well with others	☐	☐
Uses table manners	☐	☐
Respects property of others	☐	☐
Able to resolve minor conflicts	☐	☐
Accepts authority	☐	☐
Cognitive/Language Development		
Counts	☐	☐
Interested in letters and sounds (beginning reading skills)	☐	☐
Good listener	☐	☐
Follows directions	☐	☐
Makes decisions or choices	☐	☐
Sees the connection between effort and accomplishment	☐	☐
Can complete a task without distractions	☐	☐

	Observed	Not Observed

Cognitive/Language Development (*continued*)

	Observed	Not Observed
Works independently, will ask for help	☐	☐
Strives to get things right	☐	☐
Likes to learn	☐	☐

Emotional Development/Feelings

	Observed	Not Observed
Feels secure away from familiar surroundings	☐	☐
Accepts mistakes	☐	☐
Expresses individual thoughts and feelings	☐	☐
Separates easily from parents	☐	☐
Develops self-confidence	☐	☐
Greater ability to control anger/fear	☐	☐

DEVELOPMENTAL CHECKLIST
5-Year-Olds

	Observed	Not Observed
Physical Growth/Motor Development		
Takes care of personal needs (ties shoes, buttons, zips, etc)	☐	☐
Coordinates body parts (biking, swimming, etc.)	☐	☐
Cuts accurately	☐	☐
Uses pencil and scissors correctly	☐	☐
Basic grasp of right and left, but confuses them	☐	☐
Movements appear smooth	☐	☐
Walks backward	☐	☐
Skips	☐	☐
Right or left handedness is established	☐	☐
Uses glue correctly and easily	☐	☐
Social/Personal Development		
Chooses own friends, may exclude a peer	☐	☐
Plays simple table games, plays competitive games	☐	☐
Engages in group play, assigning roles, making decisions	☐	☐
Wants fair play	☐	☐
Interacts with peers and adults	☐	☐
Respects property and others	☐	☐
Leadership skills appear	☐	☐
Ability to follow peers	☐	☐
Shares, waits turn	☐	☐
Cognitive/Language Development		
Uses complete, complex sentences to express ideas	☐	☐
Records ideas using drawing, letter-like forms, invented spelling	☐	☐
Recognizes letters and some words	☐	☐
Recognizes numerals	☐	☐
Recognizes shapes	☐	☐

	Observed	Not Observed
Cognitive/Language Development (*continued*)		
Understands patterns and sequencing	☐	☐
Understands one-to-one correspondence	☐	☐
Understands categories	☐	☐
Compares, arranges in order	☐	☐
Understands positional words	☐	☐
Understands rhyming words	☐	☐
Emotional Development/Feelings		
Shows self-control	☐	☐
Separates from parents	☐	☐
Comfortable with large groups	☐	☐
Cooperative attitude	☐	☐
Resolves conflicts verbally	☐	☐
Responds well to corrections or suggestions	☐	☐

DEVELOPMENTAL CHECKLIST
6–8-Year-Olds

	Observed	Not Observed

Physical Growth/Motor Development

	Observed	Not Observed
Rate of growth slows, but growth spurts occur	☐	☐
Enjoys team sports	☐	☐
Repeats skill for mastery (bike riding, skating, swimming, etc.)	☐	☐
Forms letters and numbers well	☐	☐
Loss of teeth	☐	☐
Body develops more proportionately	☐	☐
Visual difficulties may surface	☐	☐
Shows coordination of large and small motor skills	☐	☐
Draws a person with clothes and body parts	☐	☐

Social/Personal Development

	Observed	Not Observed
Prefers own sex, less boy–girl interaction	☐	☐
Forms peer groups	☐	☐
Works and plays independently	☐	☐
Takes responsibility	☐	☐
Wants to please	☐	☐
Enjoys imaginative play	☐	☐
Works well in a group or alone	☐	☐
Communicates well/engages in conversation	☐	☐
Develops self-control	☐	☐

Cognitive/Language Development

	Observed	Not Observed
Speaks in complex sentences	☐	☐
Solves problems	☐	☐
Can distinguish fantasy from reality	☐	☐
Uses hands-on manipulatives for understanding concepts	☐	☐
Longer attention span develops	☐	☐
Interested in more knowledge of the world	☐	☐

	Observed	Not Observed
Cognitive/Language Development (*continued*)		
Differences in abilities begin to show	☐	☐
Conscious of others and compares work	☐	☐
Becoming an accomplished reader	☐	☐
Emotional Development/Feelings		
Worries	☐	☐
May show outbursts of emotions	☐	☐
Desires praise	☐	☐
Learning how to express feelings appropriately	☐	☐
Shows empathy	☐	☐
Sense of humor expands	☐	☐
Can be sensitive, has feelings hurt easily	☐	☐

Appendix B

Parent Interview Forms

PARENT INTERVIEW FORM

Beginning of the Year

Child _____ Date _____

Parent/guardian_____

To begin the conference, say the following;

Thank you for trusting me with your child this year. I know it is going to be a great year. I have already noticed that _____ loves the pets in our classroom. He must really be an animal lover.

   Parents will respond because you have opened the conversation in a positive, friendly way. You may begin with questions similar to those that follow or make up your own.

1. Tell me about your family. (Who lives in the house, how many brothers or sisters, etc.?)

2. What kinds of things do you do as a family? What things are you interested in? (Sports, music, animals, etc.) How do you spend free time as a family?

3. Do both parents work? What kinds of jobs do you have? What hours do you work?

4. What is the most important thing I need to know about your child?

5. Tell me about his/her eating and sleeping habits.

6. How do you discipline at home?

7. Could you offer some strengths and weaknesses that you see in your child?

8. Do you see your child as
   - a leader or a follower?
   - independent or dependent?
   - a contented child or an unhappy child?
   - shy or confident?
   - having self-control or lacking self-control?

At this point, you can share some strengths or positives that you have noticed. You also can state the immediate goals you have set for the child, for example:

- learning to follow two-step directions
- strengthening fine motor skills
- striving to be less argumentative during outdoor play

Goals:

To close the conference, say the following:

I would like to share some things that we will be doing in class this year because I want you to feel that you are a part of your child's activities.

At this time, have some special things ready to share about you and your classroom.

Special Things:

Please feel welcome to visit often. There will be notes posted outside the door (or sent home). I will communicate often to let you know how _____ is doing. Please send me notes or call when there is something that I need to know as well. It is going to be a good year. I am so glad you could come and visit me today. You have a precious child and I look forward to being a part of your family this year.

PARENT INTERVIEW FORM

Middle of the Year

Child _____ Date _____

Parent/guardian_____

Open the conference with a positive comment.

You know the child well, so you should have several positive things to say. Write them down.

- Have some specific items from the portfolio to share with the parents. It could be photographs, artwork, scribbling or writing samples, an audiocassette tape of their child's language development, a checklist of things he/she can do, anecdotal records, etc. Discuss each item. This is the opening for discussing problem areas as well as strengths.

- Explain that you will save these items in the portfolio, but they will be given to the parents at the end of the year. You can offer the parent a copy of the checklist if you choose to use it.

- Have a list of positive things to say about that child.

- Discuss any problems after the positive things have been mentioned. Be sure not to label the child.

- This is the time to address any problems or issues. You need to mention that the year is one-half over and specific problems may need their advice, help, and direction. You have had the child long enough to have documentation on any major issue and written documentation will be critical as you discuss, *not label,* problems. This is a good time to decide together the progress of those problem areas.

- The director of your center can be part of the conference if you feel more confident having someone of authority with you.

- End the conference on a positive comment.

Thank the parent(s) for coming and for caring.

Conference Suggestions:

What documentation will you show?

Child's strengths:

Child's weaknesses (set goals today):

Ask for any parental concerns not discussed before today.

Teacher and parent goals for the remainder of the year:

Appendix C

Sample
Anecdotal Records

Sample Anecdotes

As you observe a child playing, write short notes on 3″ x 5″ sticky notes answering some of these questions.

- What is happening?

- During center time, is the child getting along well with other children?

- What feeling or emotion is the child showing?

- During outside play, does the child have control of his body parts? Is the child coordinated as he moves?

- How well does the child communicate or talk with others? Document specific examples to show language development.

Example: *John came to school this morning crying and clinging to Mom. Later, when I asked him if something was wrong, he hit me with a block. He said, "My dog got runded over by a car last night." John is not only sad, but said he is mad at the man who hit his dog. John always has a smile on his face, but not today.*

Example: *I called the children to circle time. Lisa looked a long time for her name, walking around looking at all of the carpet squares. I had moved them from the regular places. She sat on Laura's name.*

At the end of the day, move the sticky notes to the child's folder. Keep one sheet of paper just for sticky notes so that they can be kept in order. If you keep four each month, you will have a nice documentation over the school year. You can keep notes on social interactions, emotions, academic growth, and physical growth. It will be helpful to have these written notes as you conference with parents about their child.

Appendix D

Sample Narrative Summaries

Narrative Summary

(Fictional sample of a 3-year-old end-of-year narrative summary)

Child: *Joseph*

Date: *May 31, 2001*

Physical Growth/Motor Development: Joseph is now holding a pencil correctly and often chooses to write or draw during center time. He cuts well and often helps others who have trouble cutting on the line. He is developing his large muscles in our outdoor play area by riding tricycles, climbing, and playing with the large balls. He has mastered catching the large ball after one bounce. He wants to skip and is working hard to learn.

Social/Personal Development: Joseph enjoys his time at school and enjoys playing in small groups, outside as well as inside. He actively participates in large group singing and movement activities. He plays mostly with other boys and is usually dependent on one other child in the group to make decisions. I am encouraging Joseph to make his own decisions. I have noticed that when he has a turn to be the leader for our class activities, he enjoys the position.

Cognitive/Language Development: Joseph listens attentively to stories and can retell them in great detail. He loves books and spends his indoor center time in our library and listening center with a book on tape. He works quickly at the art table so that he can move to an area where he can look at books or write. He can follow instructions and completes tasks assigned to him during the day. He is learning to be a problem solver and will try many solutions before he asks for my help.

Emotional Development/Feelings: Joseph is happy at school and is gaining self-confidence. He is kind to the others and is generous in sharing. He is slow to anger and has patience with others who cannot do all of the things in the classroom as quickly as he can.

Narrative Summary

Child: _____

Date: _____

Physical Growth/Motor Development:

Social/Personal Development:

Cognitive/Language Development:

Emotional Development/Feelings:

Glossary

The author and Delmar make every effort to ensure that all Internet resources are accurate at the time of printing. However, due to the fluid, time-sensitive nature of the Internet, we cannot guarantee that all URLs and Web site addresses will remain current for the duration of this edition.

assessment—taking stock of the situation; observation to determine growth and development.

authentic assessment—the process using real-life situations to document growth and development over time.

cognitive/language development—a developmental area that refers to the child's mental growth and development, which includes language. The word cognitive means thinking; therefore, how a child thinks is an indicator of development.

developmental checklist—an age specific list of the four key developmental areas that can be used to track a child's progress over time.

developmental milestones—basic skills or accomplishments that can be recognized in most children at a particular age. These milestones benchmark a child's progress.

emotional development/feelings—a developmental area that refers to the child's growth and development of feelings and how they are expressed. Self-esteem is also part of this area of development.

growth—the process of developing and maturing

narrative summary—a short summary, written by the teacher at the end of the year, describing a child's progress from the beginning to end of the year. This should be included in the child's portfolio to be shared with parents and the child's next teacher.

National Association for the Education of Young Children (NAEYC)—one of the most respected professional organizations in the field of early childhood education that believes that assessment helps students, teachers, and parents, as long as it is conducted in a developmentally appropriate manner <http://www.naeyc.org>.

National Education Goals Panel—a committee set up in the 1990s to research the value of assessment of young children and make recommendations on appropriate methods of assessment <http://www.negp.gov>.

observation—a method used to assess young children's growth and development through recognizing and then recording an event

performance-based assessment—an assessment based on a child's knowledge represented by physically showing or doing than by writing in a test booklet; a process, not a product.

physical growth/motor development—a developmental area that refers to the child's actual physical growth of the body as they gain ability to move and control body parts.

portfolio—a collection of items that reveals different aspects of an individual child's growth and development over time.

portfolio approach—an alternative assessment method that allows the teacher to document growth and development by collecting work and notes throughout the year.

professional portfolio—work that has been saved to document that a child has mastered particular objectives.

social/personal development—a developmental area that refers to the child's development of social skills or the ability to interact with others. It also includes how the children feel about themselves.

teacher-made portfolio—the actual container made from poster board or tag board to safely store a child's work.

working portfolio—a child's work, collected over a period of time, that is continuously changing. Teachers add to this portfolio periodically to show growth and development.

References and

Additional Readings

References

Bredekamp, S., & Copple, C. (Eds.). (1997). *Developmentally appropriate practice in early childhood programs* (Rev. ed.). Washington, DC: National Association for the Education of Young Children.

Goodenough, F. L. (1975). *Measurement of intelligence by drawings* (*Classics in child development*). North Stratford, NH: Ayer Company Publishers.

National Education Goals Panel. (1998). *National education reform leadership, standards, and assessments.* Washington, DC: U.S. Government Printing Office.

Shores, E., & Grace, C. (1998). *The portfolio book.* Beltsville, MD: Gryphon House.

Additional Readings

Adam-Bullock, A. (1998). How can I collect and use anecdotal records. *New teacher advocate.* Indianapolis, IN: Kappa Delta Pi publication.

Allen, K. E., & Marotz, L. R. (1999). *Developmental profiles: Pre-birth through eight* (3rd ed.). Albany, NY: Delmar.

Black, J., & Puckett, M. (1996). *The young child.* Englewood Cliffs, NJ: Prentice Hall.

Bredekamp, S., & Rosegrant, T. (Eds.). (1992). *Reaching potentials: Appropriate curriculum and assessment for young children* (Vol. 1). Washington, DC: National Association for the Education of Young Children.

Bredekamp, S., & Rosegrant, T. (Eds.). (1995). *Reaching potentials: Appropriate curriculum and assessment for young children* (Vol. 2). Washington, DC: National Association for the Education of Young Children.

Gronlund, G. (1998). Portfolios as an assessment tool: Is collection of work enough? *Young children, 5,* 4–10.

McDonald, S. (1997). *The portfolio and its use.* Little Rock, AR: Southern Early Childhood Association.

Miller, K. (1985). *Ages and stages.* Marshfield, MA: Telshare Publishing Co.

Pitcher, E., Feinburg, S., & Alexander, D. (1989). *Helping young children learn.* Upper Saddle River, NJ: Prentice Hall.

Seefeldt, C., & Barbour, N. (1998). *Early childhood education: An introduction.* Upper Saddle River, NJ: Prentice Hall.

Schweinhard, L. (1993). Observing young children in action: The key to early childhood assessment. *Young children, 7,* 29–33.

Texas Association for the Education of Young Children. (1997). *Assessment of young children: A position statement.* Austin, TX: Author.

Index